Living in the
New Millennium

Houses at the start of the 21st Century

Introduction 5
Living in the New Millennium

Kangaloon House 6
Glenn Murcutt

House in Ribeirão Preto 10
MMBB/SPBR

The Red House 14
Tony Fretton Architects

Roof House 18
Tezuka Architects

Casa Larrain 22
Cecilia Puga Larrain

Springtecture B House 26
Shuhei Endo Architect Institute

2-Parts House 30
BKK Architects

Casa Ponce 34
Mathias Klotz

Du Plessis House 38
Márcio Kogan

Father's House in Jade Mountains 42
MADA s.p.a.m.

Dragspel House 46
24 H-architecture

Goodman House 50
Preston Scott Cohen

Hill House 54
Johnston Marklee & Associates

Holiday House on the Rigi 58
Andreas Fuhrimann, Gabrielle Hächler Architekten

House on the Coast 62
Aires Mateus

Baron House 66
John Pawson

Brick House 70
Caruso St John Architects

Delta Shelter 74
Olson Sundberg Kundig Allen Architects

Fireworks House 78
Nendo Inc

Holman House 82
Durbach Block Architects

House in Brione 86
Markus Wespi Jérôme de Meuron Architects

House SH 90
Hiroshi Nakamura & NAP Architects

Lotus House 94
Kengo Kuma & Associates

Slice House 98
Procter:Rihl

Solar Umbrella House 102
Pugh + Scarpa Architects

St Andrews Beach House 106
Sean Godsell Architects

Tóló House 110
Alvaro Leite Siza Vieira

Wheatsheaf House 114
Jesse Judd Architects

Fink House 118
Dietrich Untertrifaller Architekten

Maison E 122
Shigeru Ban Architects

Mimetic House 126
Dominic Stevens Architect

Ring House 130
Makoto Takei + Chie Nabeshima / TNA

House in Pego 134
Siza Vieira Arquiteto

House O 138
Sou Fujimoto Architects

Villa 1 142
Powerhouse Company

Villa NM 146
UNStudio

Index 150
Picture credits 152

Living in the New Millennium

In an increasingly networked world, with its unlimited possibilities to work, socialize and travel globally, the house as a building type is evolving. During the twentieth century the act of habitation seemed to shake off its formal concerns, forging new spaces in which domestic activities could be shared, rather than contained. In the early years of the twenty-first century, this idea of integration has been extended to connections between the home and the office and between work and play. In meeting the needs of the modern client, the twenty-first century architect has to look outside the norms of residential design to embrace a new range of spatial opportunities — even creating a new language. The challenge has been to move forwards while preserving the notions that are timeless in the creation of a home: access to a world outside the domestic realm, whether that be in the city, on the coast or in the countryside.

The buildings in this book are located around the globe. Each addresses a range of issues unique to its site and to its social, cultural and economic context, and the innovative way in which these buildings deal with their individual set of constraints is especially interesting. In most cases it is a dynamic encounter between the client's wishes and the architect's creativity that has led to the commissioning of a house. The houses do not reflect a set of isolated hopes and needs. City buildings fit into the urban fabric but offer sanctuary behind closed doors. There are many references to the home as a getaway, either as a weekend retreat or something more permanent. Common to these projects is a desire to re-engage with nature. Sometimes, this is expressed in a consciously pared-down design that bucks the high-tech trend. In other cases, the landscape or seascape is there to be enjoyed in a controlled, almost cinematic way. In both scenarios a blurring of the boundaries between the built and natural worlds seems to be increasingly tied up with responsible design. Whether a house seeks to blend into its surroundings or stand apart from it, these buildings demonstrate that it is possible to create show-stopping homes with minimum ecological impact and low energy use in the long term.

The architect relies on the processes of design and construction to carry through the concept behind a building. In the new millennium, technological advances in both have led to more structurally and aesthetically daring forms. Many of the houses in this book explore the potential of new materials and building techniques to define and shape the fluid spaces that characterize modern life, especially in an urban setting. This often involves the appropriation of elements from commercial and industrial design. It is an understanding of the intrinsic qualities of materials, whether natural or synthetic, and the honesty of their application that creates excellent twenty-first century homes.

Kangaloon House
Glenn Murcutt

1

Kangaloon House

2

Set amid the rolling Southern Highlands, Kangaloon House looks north over open countryside. Although only two hours' drive from Sydney, it is common among Murcutt's buildings for its distinctly rural feel and connection to both landscape and climate. Laid out over a single storey, the two-part house sits low on its lakeside plot, protected by a curved wind deflector along its full 80 m (262.5 ft) length. From its sliding internal screens to its louvred front facade, it has the potential to be constantly 'fine tuned' to its ever changing environment.

The house comprises two wings: a main dwelling; and a small outbuilding. These are set out in a straight line along an east–west axis, with a courtyard between them. All elements are linked and protected by the wind deflector, which becomes an internal element for the main building. Connected to the house by high-level glazing, it encloses a 70 m (229 ft) long gallery off which each room is set, side by side. There are bedrooms at either end of the linear plan and shared, flexible spaces in the middle. Towards the gallery, deep walls of integrated storage provide thermal mass. To the north, sliding doors open onto a terrace.

The exact position of the house has been determined by the movement of the sun and wind relative to the large, exposed site. A bank of solar panels on the outhouse generate energy. In the main house, materials and forms (borrowed from rural building types) work in support of a naturally lit and vented interior, despite external climatic extremes. The deflector is fashioned from corrugated steel and sweeps harsh winds over the gable roof, with its large overhangs to each end. On the north face, sliding timber shutters filter strong sunlight and create a rhythmic composition together with glazing, concrete columns and a slate-tiled plinth.

1   House in context
2   West facade
3   Kitchen
4   North facade
5   Detail of wind deflector
6,7   Exterior details
8,9   Views of living space

3

4

5

6

Kangaloon, New South Wales, Australia
2000

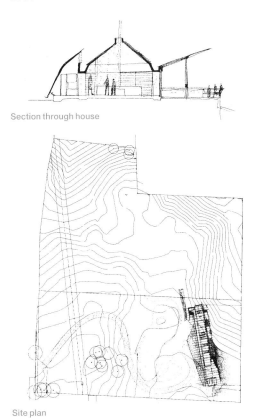

Section through house

Site plan

7

8

9

House in Ribeirão Preto
MMBB / SPBR

Situated in southern Brazil, Ribeirão Preto is a wealthy city known colloquially as the 'Brazilian California'. Its temperate climate is ideally suited to the light-filled architecture of MMBB and SPBR, both youthful practices with close ties to the University of São Paulo. Designed as a courtyard-style residence for a family, the House in Ribeirão Preto shows the influence of what is known as 'brutalist' architecture. It is geometric and celebrates both the structural and aesthetic possibilities of concrete, in particular its ability to support column-free interiors and large areas of glazing.

The building is principally laid out over a single storey just above ground level. U-shaped in plan, it sits on four slender concrete columns. These are set into a series of cavities carved out of a levelled suburban plot. Entry is by way of an external staircase rising up from basement level, where cars can be parked under one wing of the house. The stairs lead to a kitchen centred on a high-sided 'island' which creates a natural corridor between public and private areas. To the north, away from the street, there are three bedrooms, bathrooms and a study. To the south, with frameless views onto a terrace, is a large open-plan living area.

Most of the house's envelope is fully glazed, which gives the building a sense of elegant weightlessness. The load-bearing elements are the four concrete columns, upper and lower horizontal slabs and up-stand beams at roof level.

Minimal partitions define the three bedrooms and bathrooms, which are masked from the exterior by a mix of translucent and steel panels. Otherwise, the courtyard layout invites views both into and through the house, causing passersby to marvel over the audacious structural approach.

1   View of main residence
2   Stairs to entrance
3   Kitchen
4,5 Details of concrete structure
6   Cor-Ten Panels on facade
7   View from pool
8,9 Interior views

3

4

5

6

7

8

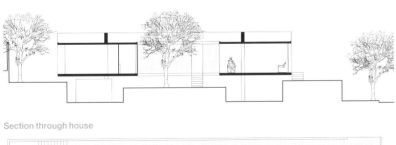

Section through house

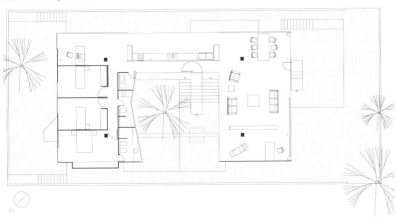

Floor plan

9

The Red House
Tony Fretton Architects

1

2

London, UK
2001

The Red House is the home of a young art collector, commissioned as both residence and workplace. Integrated into a historic London streetscape, it has been designed to engage with its urban context in a way that is respectful but self-assured. Through the formal composition and stonework of its main facade, it enters into an ongoing dialogue with its setting, encouraging comparison and adding to the cultural life of the city. As a gallery and future family home, it sits neatly within the architect's wider portfolio, a flexible building with a versatile interior.

The house draws on the arrangement of neighbouring buildings and is scaled to its setting. It is laid out over three main floors (plus basement and mezzanine) and is largely contained within a square footprint, save for a glazed dining pavilion on the ground floor. The prevailing sense of order provides a framework for the interior, which has been designed in collaboration with artist-architect Mark Pimlott and will evolve over time to meet the owner's needs. Largely free of prescribed functionality, each floor has unique spatial qualities and character, and there is a carefully orchestrated interplay between shared and intimate spaces.

The house is of reinforced concrete construction, which gives the interior a lightness of touch behind the solid stone facade. The rich red cladding, after which the house is named, is a textured French limestone, chosen for its natural beauty, historical provenance and durability. Glazing is used extensively and with characteristic contrast, juxtaposing windows that have bronze and timber surrounds with large areas of frameless screening. The garden elevation is more open than the street, providing light to the upper-level bedroom pavilions and views over to Sir Christopher Wren's Royal Hospital and, beyond, Westminster Cathedral.

1   Exterior from street
2   Stairs leading from dining area
3,4   Red stone facade
5   First floor interior
6,7   Views of living space
8   Detail of French limestone
9   View from garden

3

4

5

6

7

8

9

Section through house

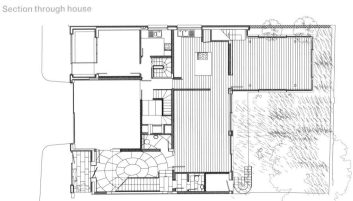

Ground-floor plan

Roof House
Tezuka Architects

1

2

Roof House aptly describes a contemporary Japanese home in which the essentials of family life are supported within and above the building. The concept stems from a light-hearted conversation about the client's alfresco lunching habits. Situated in a modern city suburb, the building encourages social living and explores the roof's potential to serve core residential functions. A theme that Tezuka develops in later buildings, this takes limitless space to a logical conclusion, merging inside with outside and — on this particular site — securing spectacular valley views.

Within the Roof House, the plan is very simple and affords optimum flexibility. It centres on a generous open-plan living space and a sequence of three private rooms to the rear. The compact kitchen and bathroom are tucked away to one side, while a wall of walk-in storage buffers sound from the road. The lightweight, timber structure allows for extensive glazing, so the private areas remain light and airy. Indeed — with the use of retractable partitions — they can be opened up completely to form one large, sociable space with views straight through the house.

The understated simplicity of the house draws attention to the rooftop and its creative new role as the hub of activity. The deck itself is a thin membrane of galvanized steel on timber panelling. Gently pitched to follow the contour of the site, it naturally orientates towards the views that extend all the way over to Mount Kobo. Its open plan is interspersed with a total of eight skylights, which are key to both physical and visual linkage. With ladders down into different internal zones, the hatches serve specific family members. This reflects the concerns of both architect and client — a strong sense of identity within an all-encompassing natural order.

1,2   Roof terrace and seating
3   Living space
4   Exterior from street
5   View through interior
6   Rooftop dining area
7   Detail of bathroom

3

4

5

6

7

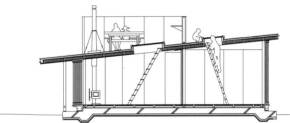

Section through house

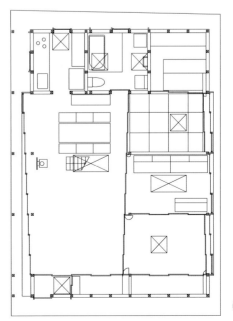

Floor plan

Casa Larrain
Cecilia Puga Larrain

Bahía Azul, Los Vilos, Chile
2002

Casa Larrain is a home for the architect's mother and a weekend retreat for her extended family. It represents the putting down of roots after many years travelling, so there is a conscious symbolism in its powerful solidity. Set on a rocky shoreline in central Chile, it is designed as a stepping-stone to the sea, with an abundance of outdoor space and expansive, carefully framed views. Through considered layout and structural ambition it achieves visual harmony and a feeling of togetherness, while maintaining discrete domestic functions and a sense of personal privacy.

The building comprises three reinforced-concrete double-pitched pavilions linked by a single horizontal truss. This has enabled the architect to place the volumes in the staggered and stacked formation that gives the house its remarkable profile and to realize her vision of a single extruded form.

There are two pavilions at ground level, with a deliberate gap between them. At the north end, the kitchen-dining pavilion terminates in a large picture window and opens onto a terrace through sliding glazed doors. To the south, there is a dormitory block. The third pavilion is an open-plan living room, again with a framed sea view. It slots into the crevice formed between the two volumes below, both of which it overlaps, and is linked to the kitchen-diner by a spiral staircase. Full-height windows add rhythm to the facades, creating visual connections across the pavilions and linking rooms with the landscape. Within the house the dominant design feature is the nakedness of the structural concrete. This creates a continuity with the exterior and sets up a non-hierarchical relationship between the various surfaces, staircase and even fixtures such as the kitchen island. The intent is the merging of structure, colour and texture to create a unified whole resonant with the spirit of the Larrain family.

1   North facade
2   House in context
3   Living room on first floor
4   Patio on west side of house
5   Patio overlooking coast
6   View of interior

3

4

5

6

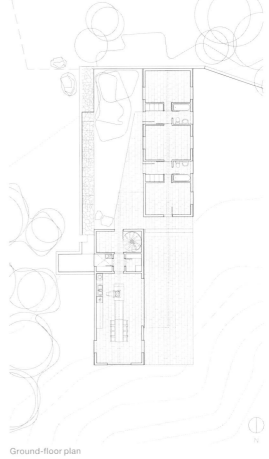

Ground-floor plan

Springtecture B House
Shuhei Endo
Architect Institute

Springtecture B is a weekend house and studio in the lakeside town of Biwa-cho. A small and highly personal project for Shuhei Endo, it explores the use of an overtly industrial material and the idea of continuity of surface applied to the emerging 'live/work' building type. It typifies the architect's 'non-compositional' approach to design, in which buildings are treated as single entities that cannot be broken down into separate parts. In particular, it represents a group of projects that use corrugated steel in dynamic folding formations to suggest constant movement and spatial flux.

Endo likens the process of design to *renmentai*, a Japanese calligraphic style in which entire texts are written in a single unbroken brushstroke. In plan, he has laid out Springtecture B in a zigzag that complements its sinuous profile. The ribbon of interlocking spaces is arranged sequentially, taking in both indoor and outdoor features as it weaves its way across the site, either side of a central spine. The freedom of the approach is suited to a house that is only for short-term occupation and which is centred on a double-height gallery and open, sociable spaces such as the poolside dining room.

The building's single continuous movement is expressed using conjoined sheets of corrugated steel to define space. Not only eye-catching, the metal strip is lightweight, economical and curves without losing strength. These qualities make it suited to the purpose of softening corners between walls, floors and ceilings. It also gives the building a lightness of touch, which is accentuated by the use of extensive glazing. Where privacy is needed, it is achieved through the positioning of key walls, such as the central plane of black and white bricks. Otherwise, the emphasis is on the generous through-movement of views, light and air.

1   East facade
2   View from northeast
3   Enclosed living space
4   South facade
5   House in context
6,7 Details of pipes supporting metal frame
8   View of interior

3

4

5

6

7

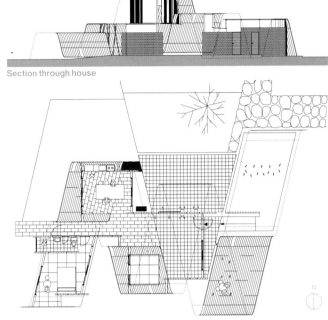

Section through house

Ground-floor plan

8

2-Parts House
BKK Architects

1

2

3

4

Melbourne, Victoria, Australia
2003

2-Parts House is a building that explores ideas of spatial duality and flux within a contemporary suburban family home. Extended from a California Bungalow — a popular coastal housing type in 1920s Australia — it creates a playful 'conversation' between its two seemingly distinct halves, a concept referencing the Victorian love seat. Over a single storey and garden, it provides a range of spaces to support the dynamics of modern family life. In some parts cellular, in others open-plan, it balances intimate with shared spaces, inside with outside.

The plan of the house is straightforward, with the extension laid out along the same central axis as the existing house. Moving from west to east, the idea of enclosure ebbs and flows depending on the function of the various spaces. Fluidity is maintained by the clear sightlines, particularly across the kitchen, dining and terrace areas. These are transitional places. They mediate between the orthogonal and irregular parts of the plan, creating a dialogue between old and new. In daily use they provide the flexibility needed to accommodate different modes of casual living.

From the positioning of the house on site to the choice of materials, the architect has sought to maximize natural resources and create a building that is energy-efficient in the long term. Both parts of the extension are timber framed and clad with a tactile double skin of untreated silvertop ash. The outer layer is applied as thin vertical batons, creating an illusion of height and providing a counterpoint to the brick of the existing house. The bulging, angular walls of the library do not merely create the building's signature sculptural form, they also allow for the long slot windows to be arranged diagonally, to track the sun's path. This harnesses daylight for longer and creates a warm internal ambience.

1   Exterior from east
2   New volume containing living space
3   North facade
4   Bookshelves between slit windows
5   Detail of north facade
6,7 Living space

31

5

6

7

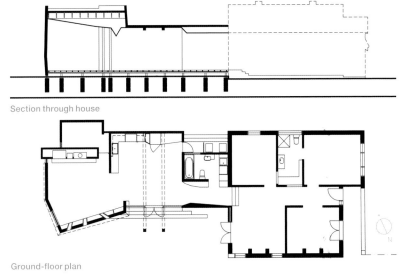

Section through house

Ground-floor plan

Casa Ponce
Mathias Klotz

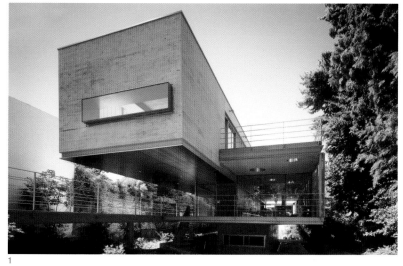

Casa Ponce is a family home in a genteel area of historic San Isidro. It is located on the banks of the Río de la Plata and occupies a long, narrow site amid lush vegetation. The commission was an ideal one for Mathias Klotz, whose portfolio is built around the idea of belonging, as it reflects a strong sense of place. Working closely with the client, Klotz's primary aim was to preserve an open view of the river, ensuring that the house did not have a divisive impact on the natural setting but became a conduit between waterfront and road.

The house is conceived as two floating volumes perched above a discreet and compact basement. Klotz has exploited the possibilities of a reinforced concrete structure to create a sense of dynamic equilibrium between the different parts, based on a strict underlying order. The living spaces have been organized into two distinct zones: open-plan and public; enclosed and private. The building's graceful profile is created by placing the more closed volume uppermost, counterbalancing a delicate glass box beneath. The apparent defiance of gravity is most marked at the river end, where the swimming pool is suspended over the sloping garden.

The ordered linearity of the plan is emphasized in the use of horizontal ribbon glazing (both translucent and transparent) to the facades and the exposure of supporting columns. A limited palette of materials has been used honestly, with the concrete of the structure left bare both inside and out.

The integration of elements into a coherent whole is supported by intricate details, such as the round rooflights on the terrace with views down into the living zone. The projection of terracing beyond the footprint extends the analogy of the building as a conversation between the garden, the river and the neighbouring streetscape.

1,2 Cantilever over pathway
3 Living space looking onto terrace
4 Entrance to house
5,6 Views of dining area
7 Interior corridor
8 Bathroom
9 Detail of roof terrace

3

4

5

6

San Isidro, Buenos Aires, Argentina
2003

7

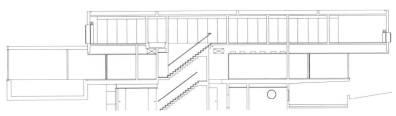

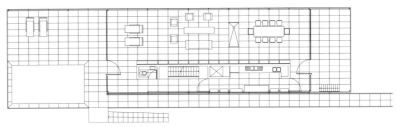

Section through house

Floor plan

8

9

Du Plessis House
Márcio Kogan

Set in a gated community near the historic city of Paraty, the Du Plessis House is one of a number of properties Márcio Kogan has designed for Laranjeiras Condominium, an extensive leisure complex surrounded by sea, mountains and rainforest. This environment has allowed the architect to work outside the constraints of the urban context and to think in more open terms about the relationship of buildings to the landscape. The project has, however, its own parameters, challenging Kogan to work within the condominium aesthetic without compromising his modernist thinking.

The house is a four-bedroom villa laid out over one floor. The architectural concept is described by Kogan as 'double face': a traditional, low-rise house is set within an open modernist box, striking a careful balance between contemporary and conventional. The solidity of the outer envelope gives protection to the inner arrangement, which incorporates two outdoor terraces and a swimming pool. It also allows for the use of more delicate facades connecting inside with outside, enabling natural ventilation and a free-flowing approach to space.

Properties in Laranjeiras are required to have colonial-style pitched roofs with clay tiles. Kogan has incorporated clay into a wider palette of natural materials that creates harmony through contrast. The shell of local Mineira stone is not intended to hide the house, as wide openings frame abstracted views out to the landscape and back into the building.

Indeed, below the parapet, the east elevation is fully retractable. There is a playful relationship between dominant forms, particularly to the south of the plan. By day, the stone exterior and court-yard jaboticaba trees predominate. At night, the building's permeable veil of recycled wood is back-lit from within, trans-forming the trees into ghostly silhouettes.

1   View from south
2   Detail of exterior
3   Living room and pool at night
4,5 Openings in exterior stone wall
6   Timber screen
7   View of living space
8,9 Pool and adjacent seating area

3

4

5

6

7

8

9

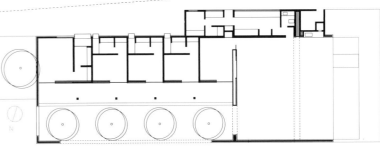

Floor plan

Father's House
in Jade Mountains
MADA s.p.a.m.

Father's House marks the return of architect Qingyun Ma to the ancient Chinese province of his birth. It is one of a number of buildings he has designed in Jade Valley, where the Qinling Mountains meet the Bahe River. This is agricultural terrain, worked by farmers with a strong sense of community and tradition. To build a house here is an important social statement and Ma has responded in a way that combines the rationale of his western training with a commitment to local techniques and materials.

The building draws on themes common to both traditional Chinese house design and the modernist movement: the relationship between indoors and outdoors, private and public. The structure comprises an outer shell and an inner skeleton, between which are a walled courtyard to the south and an ornamental pool to the east. While the shell is solid, the skeleton is filled in with a mixture of transparent and opaque panels. This makes it easy to appreciate the disciplined, modular layout of the two-storey space within. Behind a ribbon of shutters, the south facade is the most open. Sliding glazed doors on the ground floor and full-height windows above create links to the courtyard from the living area and upper master bedroom.

Ma is known for his hands-on approach to construction and careful selection of materials. In Father's House he uses stones from a nearby river both on the outer envelope and in the concealed parts of the facades. The project took five years to complete, as it was built by local residents who hand-picked and sorted each stone according to size, shape and colour. The result is a rich textural contrast between the smooth rounded stonework and crisply detailed glazing. Inside, this is beautifully offset by the finely latticed panels of woven bamboo on plywood.

1   House in context
2   Garden facade
3   Ornamental pool
4   Garden facade glass doors and shutters
5   View of living space
6   Detail of interior

3

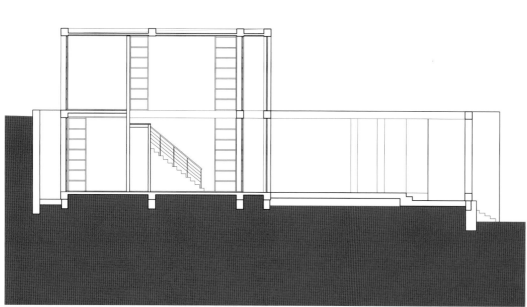

Section through house

4

5

Dragspel House
24 H-architecture

Årjäng, Sweden
2004

Dragspel House is an extension to a fishing cabin, creating a small holiday home for the architects on an idyllic lakeside plot. Its design is a creative response to strict regulations governing the size of buildings in the protected nature reserve in which it is set. It is a template project in terms of its impact on site, energy use and respect for the beauty of its natural surroundings. It responds readily to environmental changes, with the ability to adjust size, shape and appearance, depending on the weather and the needs of its users over the course of their stay.

The extension functions as an open-plan living space with a small island kitchen. Accessed from the existing cabin through one small opening, it is a timber-framed structure made up of twenty-seven individually shaped ribs. These link the main volume (which is the maximum size permitted for the site) with a smaller section that extends and retracts on rollers. At full reach, the house projects over an adjacent stream and opens up to the site through four large windows. Its sinuous shape is driven by the irregular rib-cage and emphasized in the waves of its western red cedar shingle skin. When closed for the winter, it becomes a cocoon, with no openings visible from the lakeside.

The house is almost fully carbon neutral. Its frame and interior pine finishes are made from locally sourced and certified wood. The cedar skin is untreated and will weather over time to the colour of nearby rocks. In the sliding portion, the walls are lined with reindeer hides, which provide a sensuous feel and excellent insulation. The chimney of a wood-fuelled stove penetrates the skin like a horn, conjuring up an image of the building as a reptilian creature that is highly attuned to its natural habitat.

1   View of exterior
2   House seen from lake
3   Living space
4   Exterior view of extended section
5   Detail of wood-clad exterior
6   Deck overlooking lake
7   Detail of an 'eye window'
8,9 Views of living space

3

4

5

6

7

8

9

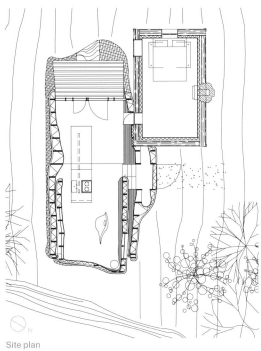

Site plan

Goodman House
Preston Scott Cohen

The Goodman House is a 'building within a building' and a radical interpretation of a traditional gabled house. Its inner core is the antique timber skeleton of a nineteenth-century Dutch barn, protected by a contemporary steel frame and a textured wooden skin. By its sheer size, it has allowed the architect to examine structure, geometry and space on an unusually grand scale for a residential project. It develops the concerns of his academic research (he is a professor at Harvard) by challenging perceived ideas about the limits of construction and a functional brief.

As clients, the Goodmans were very informed about modern architecture and were clear in their desire for a spacious open-plan home with as much natural light as possible. The challenge was to accommodate their needs within the context of the Dutch barn, which they loved for its tactile and spatial qualities. The architect has responded with a layered composition that not only puts the different structural components on show but draws specific attention to them. From the outside, glimpses of both the timber and offset steel structures are invited through the forty-eight differently sized windows that scatter the facades. There is a deliberate contrast between the expanse of the elevations and their delicate cladding of tongue-and-groove cedar boards.

The freedom of the structure is most apparent where a breezeway slices right through the house, turning it momentarily 'inside out'. Through the use of sliding screens and roll-down glass doors, the tunnel becomes a winter garden, bringing a taste of the rural surroundings indoors. This adds to a rich and varied interior characterized by contrasts of materials and scale — rustic and refined, large and small. Pockets of bathing and sleeping space are discreetly laid out to one side, thus preserving the impact of the cathedral-like skeletal barn.

1   House in context
2   Southeast facade
3   View of living space
4   Open-ended hallway forming main entrance
5   Main living space
6   Dining area looking onto kitchen

3

4

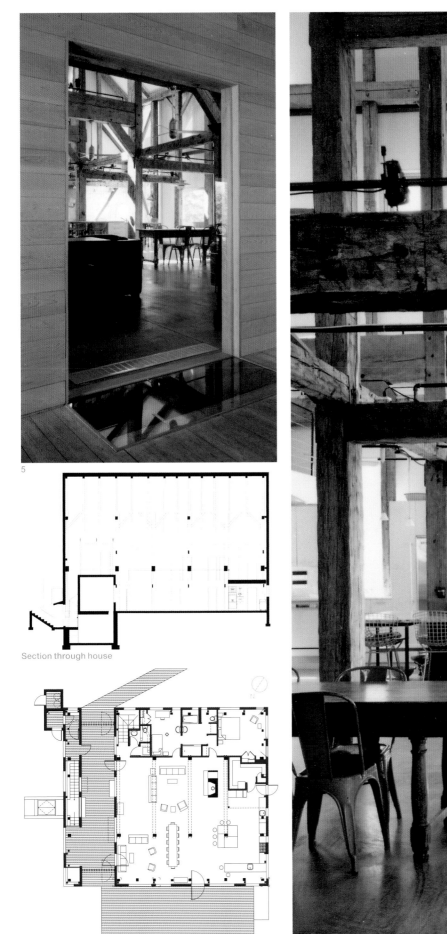

5

Section through house

Ground-floor plan

6

Hill House
Johnston Marklee
& Associates

Santa Monica, California, USA
2004

Hill House is situated on one of the most iconic building strips in modern residential architecture. Perched on the edge of Chautauqua Boulevard, it shares its magnificent outlook over Santa Monica Canyon with Case Study House No. 8 by Charles and Ray Eames. Undoubtedly a prime plot for development, it nonetheless presented particular challenges to the architects in designing a contemporary family home for the site. Not only was it steep and uneven, but it was also subject to stringent height and massing conditions imposed by local building regulations.

From the outset the architect approached the restrictions of the site as a structural and spatial opportunity. The prescribed zoning envelope was fully investigated to determine what it could offer in terms of maximum usable space and minimum environmental impact. It was then adopted as the building form and the structure developed to make it buildable. The resulting volume has a folded sculptural quality and engages with its site as if it were hewn out of the rocky terrain. The distinction between walls and roof planes has been blurred so that they read as one continuous surface. The tapered lower reaches allow the building to be read from below as well as from the road above.

The monumental quality of Hill House is heightened by the deep recessing of openings on the two private levels, in contrast to the middle public level where full-height glass doors retract to reveal breathtaking views and allow optimum natural light and ventilation to the predominantly white interior. The structure itself is a braced steel frame infilled with timber and anchored on a concrete base. It is a highly efficient skeleton that supports a free-flowing, open-plan layout, dramatic cantilevering and connectivity via a sculptural feature staircase.

1,2   Views of exterior
3   View of living space
4,5   Details of exterior
6,7   Ground-floor living space
8,9   Mezzanine level

3

55

4

5

6

7

8

9

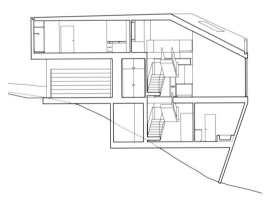

Section through house

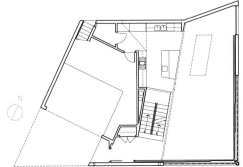

Upper-level plan

Holiday House on the Rigi
Andreas Fuhrimann,
Gabrielle Hächler Architekten

The Rigi Scheidegg is known as the 'Queen of the Mountains' and is a popular mountain resort an hour from Zürich. With views that captivated the English painter J. M. W. Turner, it makes the perfect setting for the shared holiday home of architect-clients Andreas Fuhrimann and Gabrielle Hächler. On its wooded slopes they have created the ideal conditions for enjoying the landscape with a designer's eye. Their airy house achieves a variety of moods and spaces through simple shifts in level, a skewed plan, a mix of rough and smooth materials, and the strategic use of apertures.

The building is located on the edge of a sloping site, as far as possible from adjacent houses. To maximize space and create a varied interior, it is an irregular kite-shape that bulges outwards in two directions. The timber-framed structure is anchored by a concrete utility basement, from which rises a chimney piercing all three levels. On the ground floor a monumental fireplace forms the building's backbone and hides the slender staircase up to the bedrooms. The flexible plan accommodates changes in level, with a stepped living room and a low-ceilinged kitchen reminiscent of mountain huts.

Fuhrimann and Hächler are fascinated with the crossover between art, architecture and design. In their weekend retreat, they have carefully sized and positioned windows to provide a shifting perspective on the majestic scenery. To the north, where the ground rises steeply, there are only four small openings in an otherwise solid wooden skin. To the west, sliding glazed partitions, directed on specific vistas, access an outdoor terrace. It is to the south, though, where the drama really unfolds. Here, a 5 m (16.4 ft) long ribbon window frames and abstracts an incredible panorama, which can be enjoyed from integrated seating and an interior rich with contrasting textures and surfaces.

1,2   Exterior views showing Alpine setting
3   Living space
4   External deck
5,6   Panoramic views from interior
7,8   Views of upper floor
9   Detail of staircase

3

4

5

6

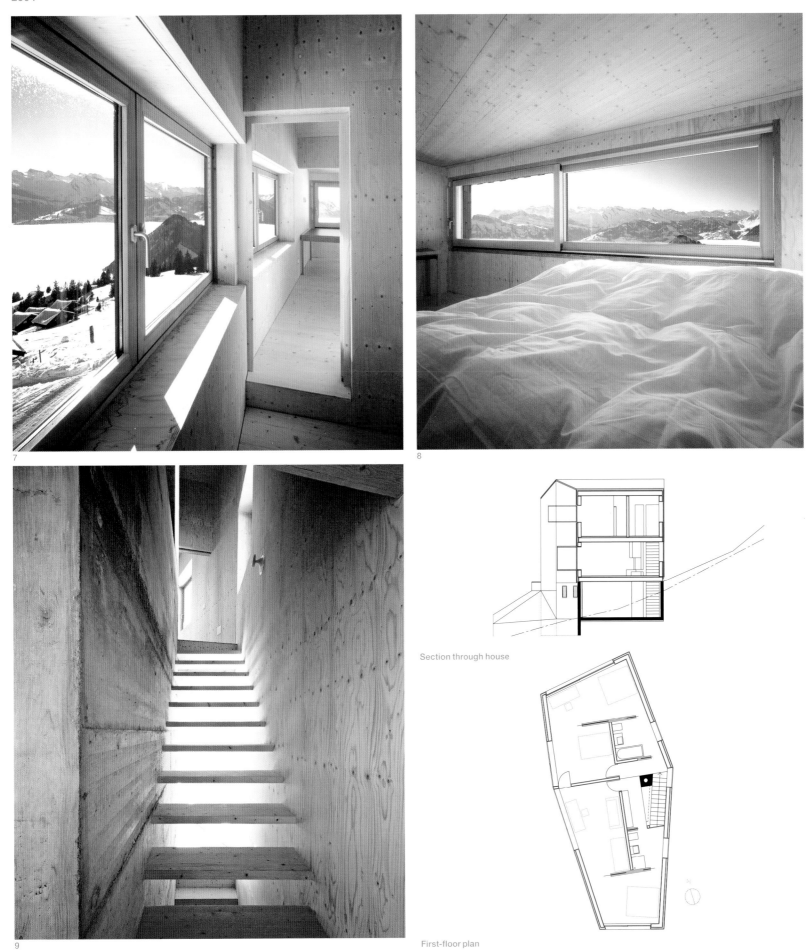

7

8

9

Section through house

First-floor plan

House on the Coast
Aires Mateus

1

2

3

In recent years, new Portuguese architecture has been predominantly focused on the country's western seaboard. In the southwest region, in particular, it is heavily influenced by the simple whitewashed cottages found along the rural coastline. Enduring the harsh Iberian sun, these buildings set a precedent in designing for hot countries and exposed coastal conditions. In this house on the Alentejo coast, Aires Mateus develops the principles behind these dwellings for the twenty-first century, producing a new rural house type that is uniquely of its place yet universally relevant.

The house is part of a development of four summer homes based around an outdoor pool. With a square plan typical of Aires Mateus, it is laid out over a single storey, giving it a strong horizontal emphasis. Only two openings pierce its blank white-rendered facades — one to the east and one to the west. This cool minimalism complements the landscape and the local style. It hides a complex asymmetric interior that is designed as if carved out of a solid, leaving thick white walls behind. Within the labyrinth, the interlocking spaces include perimeter bedrooms and bathrooms, a kitchen and an open-plan living area. These are interspersed with four small patios and a central walled courtyard.

House on the Coast explores the idea of the power of suggestion in architecture. In keeping with the vernacular, it uses limited means to create subtle changes in mood and regulate temperature.

When sliding wooden shutters close the outer envelope, sunlight and fresh air still filter in through the patios and courtyard. Likewise, when pivoting glazed walls open the bedrooms (to create flexible space with the living area), privacy is not sacrificed. Instead, it is maintained by the clever combination of raised floors, lowered ceilings and the strategic placement of crisp white partitions.

1   Sunken pool
2,3 West facade showing sliding patio door
4   View of patio with sliding door
5   View of exterior
6,7 Details of patio
8,9 Details of interior

4

West elevation

Floor plan

5

6

7

8

9

Baron House
John Pawson

1

2

3

4

Skåne, Sweden
2005

Baron House is a holiday home built on the site of a traditional farmstead, amid rolling fields of wheat and barley. A collection of pitched-roofed volumes around a central courtyard, the house draws heavily on the character of local buildings. While large, it does not dominate the landscape and retains a sense of privacy and human scale. Through the considered use of materials, precise detailing and carefully controlled views, it is a light and airy home that provides a contemporary precedent for housing in a rural setting.

In defining the brief for their new house, the clients were keen that their enjoyment of the landscape should not have an impact on the site's ecology. This fed into the concept of the building

as a series of four low-rise interlocking volumes with simple white walls, dark timber shuttering and silver pitched roofs. The design retains the general arrangement of the former farm buildings and is laid out over one ground-floor level plus a small basement. It is organized into two main wings: one shared and open-plan; one private and enclosed. These are linked by an entrance breezeway with long views across the central courtyard.

The interior of the house continues the understated look of the exterior. Rooms are plastered plain white, floors are poured concrete and meticulous attention has been paid to details such as angular integrated furniture. The effect is one of abstraction that artfully plays with ideas of perception and

scale. It allows the building to derive its drama from the effect of light on surfaces and carefully chosen materials, rather than colour and a broad range of textures. The principal interior design tool is in fact the rolling landscape, which is captured like a picture through large frameless windows.

1   House in context
2   Living space
3   Detail of facade
4   Dining area
5   View from northeast
6   View into courtyard
7   View of living space from exterior
8   Bathroom

Baron House
John Pawson

5

6

7

8

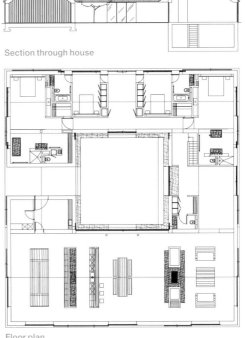

Section through house

Floor plan

Brick House
Caruso St John Architects

2

London, UK
2005

On an overlooked end-of-terrace plot nestled among a dense network of houses, Brick House is a family home specifically designed to foster communal living. Its unique plan and folded, angular profile derive from the odd shape of its 'leftover' site and issues of light and privacy. With no elevations to the street, the house is an unannounced presence in the fashionable London neighbourhood of Notting Hill. It is instead focused on a vibrant central living area, in which space, light and form have been drawn inwards and a single, familiar material predominates in creating a cohesive family environment.

The building occupies two floors: upper ground; and lower. Its plan is loosely triangular, with a courtyard at each peripheral corner. Although

unconventional in design terms, the asymmetric layout responds to the social norms of family living. It places the kitchen upstairs at the hub of activity, with direct access to dining and lounge areas. Collectively these form the building's communal heart — a flexible, open-plan space with a lofty ceiling height in the central portion. Utility and plant are secreted downstairs, which is a private zone arranged in cellular form. It incorporates a master suite and three further bedrooms, each with access to a courtyard.

The house is largely made of brick, inside and out. Together with the free-flowing plan, it is the predominance of this single, highly-tactile material that gives the building its sense of togetherness.

Used on both floors and walls, subtle delineation is achieved by the detail of how the bricks are arranged within the mortar. This achieves spatial continuity and the sense of the building as a single object somehow carved out of a mass. The effect is enhanced by the cast concrete ceiling, specifically its exposed depth over the dining area and perforation by dramatic, sculptural lightwells.

1   Street facade
2   Kitchen area
3   Second bedroom courtyard
4   Entrance
5   Ground-floor hall
6   Master Bedroom

3

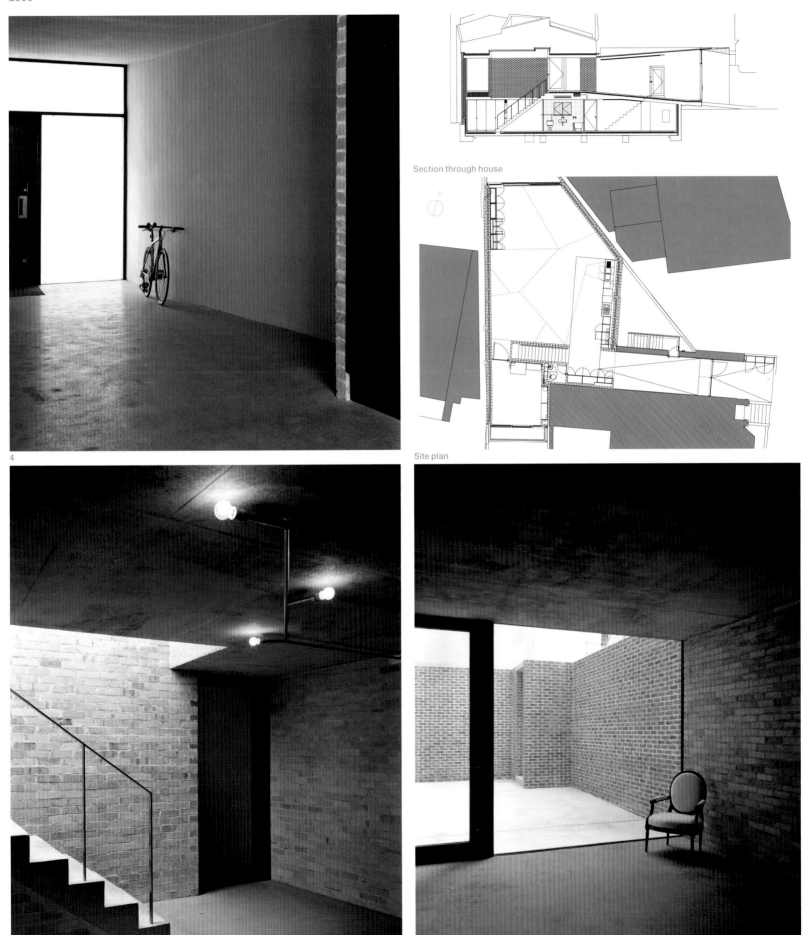

London, UK
2005

Section through house

Site plan

4

5

6

Delta Shelter
Olson Sundberg Kundig
Allen Architects

1

2

Mazama, Washington, USA
2005

The Delta Shelter is a small weekend retreat set in an isolated valley among the stunning Cascade Mountains. Commissioned by a sporting enthusiast as a base camp for skiing and hiking, its primary function is to provide overnight protection from the elements. It is deliberately low tech and low impact: a quiet, unassuming building that draws attention away from itself towards the wider landscape. It slots into its alpine surroundings like an intricate piece of a larger jigsaw — a metaphor taken forward in the use of sliding shutters to screen all openings when the building is not in use.

The shelter is a deceptively simple building that belies the careful consideration given to its design and siting. Its form is compact and economic, with a minimal footprint of 18.5 m² (200 sq ft). Raised above ground on stilts, it is protected against damage from vandalism and the surrounding flood plain. It rests lightly on site with minimum ecological impact and enjoys sweeping panoramic views from full-height windows. There are two main levels of accommodation: bedrooms and bathroom on the first floor; kitchen and living on the second.

The shelter is exceptionally efficient and virtually indestructible. A limited palette of materials has been used with integrity, creating an interesting dynamic between built form and landscape. The steel structure was largely prefabricated off-site and one half of each facade can be fully opened up to naturally ventilate the interior, where low-grade plywood is the predominant finish. A clerestory allows daylight in, even when the main windows have been screened. The shutters themselves are closed using a hand-wheel and pulleys that drag the four large steel panels across the facades. They 'close' the house, achieving an anonymity for the building that is both a safeguard and a final note of reverence to the landscape.

1,2   Views of exterior
3   Living space
4   House in winter
5,6   Exterior sliding panel
7   View of entrance
8,9   Details of interior

3

Delta Shelter
Olson Sundberg Kundig Allen Architects

4

5

6

7

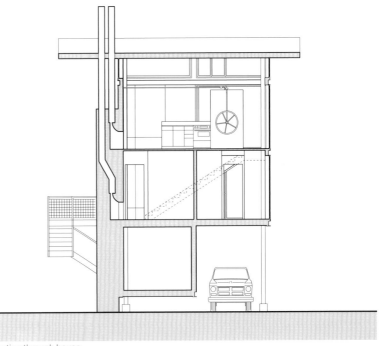

Section through house

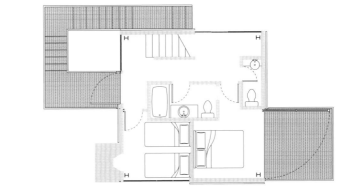

First-floor plan

N

8

9

Fireworks House
Nendo Inc

Commissioned for an elderly client, Fireworks House was built for an annual Chichibu celebration. As a vehicle for a grandmother to enjoy the *Yomatsuri* (Night Festival) with her family, it epitomizes the people-friendly portfolio of Nendo Inc, a young multidisciplinary practice. The architect's aim has been to create an intimate home that precisely meets its owner's needs. The challenge has been to provide, for a wheelchair user, an unparalleled view of the night sky and to create a sociable family space that also feels comfortable when the client is alone.

Chichibu is set in mountainous terrain and is steeped in religious history. Nendo's house exploits the hilly site to provide a viewing platform for the fireworks festival, which honours a Buddhist deity. The building is small — a little under 120 m² (1291 sq ft) — and has a simple timber framework, which reflects both local construction methods and the limited budget. Like neighbouring houses, it is of modest proportion and its compact layout is largely focused on the ground floor. This everyday level is arranged as a ring of accessible open-plan living spaces around a central utility core. By contrast, the upstairs mezzanine is a narrow observation deck that requires assisted access.

The building is clad in industrial matt grey steel finished with a brickwork pattern. This playfully challenges ideas about what a domestic building should look like. Inside, the timber structure is exposed and the walls are finished in rough wood.

With no windows onto surrounding streets at pavement level, it is the pitched roof that opens up to the sky through large apertures. These bring in natural light and create a stunning frame for the firework display. Although the roof is steeply raked, it is suited to the suburban context: like the building as a whole, it creates a bold visual statement while respecting regional character.

1   View of exterior
2   South facade
3   Detail of viewing platform
4   View of living space
5,6 Details of staircase and roofspace
7   Roofspace

3

4

5

6

7

Section through house

Ground-floor plan

Holman House
Durbach Block Architects

Dover Heights, New South Wales, Australia
2005

Holman House occupies a prime cliff-top location in an affluent Sydney suburb, commanding Pacific Ocean views on three sides. Making the most of this superb panorama underpins every facet of the building, from concept through to detail. The signature curves free the plan from the strict geometry of the suburban grid, creating a relationship with the ocean that appropriately ebbs and flows. The natural profile of protrusions and recesses claims pockets of liveable outdoor space that are protected from full coastal exposure and the hubbub of suburban activity.

The house is laid out over two floors, each offering an entirely different environment. The lower level is a secluded, private zone comprising bathrooms, guest bedrooms and utility areas. It is a compact volume in rough stone and recedes in plan, anchoring the house to the cliff. In marked contrast, the upper level is an open, fluid space that cartwheels out from a central kitchen area. It is stretched across the width of the site, with an undulating perimeter that forks out into the ocean before curling back in on itself. The sequence of living spaces provides a changing cinematic experience of the seascape, with framed full-height windows to the north and south, and a slotted glazed ribbon window to the east.

Continuing the plan's formal concerns, Durbach Block have used construction techniques and materials to explore further the relationship between 'push' and 'pull'. The living and dining wings are dramatically cantilevered over the cliff edge, supported on slender stilts. A sliding glass door opens onto a north-facing courtyard, which sweeps towards the interior on a bed of blue-grey slate. The lower walls extend into those of a terraced landscaped garden, which incorporates a swimming pool. Throughout, the emphasis is on capturing the best light, air and views through an interdependence of building and site.

1,2   Views of exterior
3   View of exterior terrace
4   Living area with ocean views
5,6   Kitchen and living area

3

83

4

Durbach Block Architects

5

6

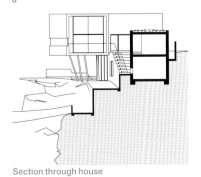

Section through house

Ground-floor plan

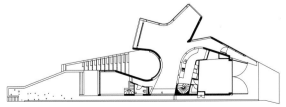

First-floor plan

House in Brione
Markus Wespi Jérôme de Meuron Architects

1

2

Brione, Locarno, Switzerland
2005

Brione, a district of the town of Locarno with a large number of detached houses, displays a suburban character. On its slopes, up-market holiday homes built in a range of styles compete for the best views of the mountains, the town and Lake Maggiore. This house by Swiss architects Marcus Wespi and Jérôme de Meuron offers a measured reaction to the surrounding visual diversity in its simple form.

The house is strikingly rectilinear. Its highly textured walls, built from local stone, appear to emerge from the hillside, connecting the house with the natural environment. Its two cubic volumes are on different tiers of the sloping site and are set perpendicular to one another in an L-shape. The upper block sits back from the valley, parallel with its contours. Here the main residential functions are arranged as open-plan living on the ground floor and bedrooms above. The lower element is a partially sunken garage with a swimming pool above.

The interior of the building has been conceived as a series of habitable spaces hollowed out of the stone. Pierced only by two openings (with sliding wooden grilles), the solid outer walls give no clue to the complexity of the spaces within. The defining element is where the two blocks meet, producing a cavernous void with a slanting concrete roof.

In a simple but considered gesture, a slotted opening provides strong directional light while diffused rays filter down from an internal courtyard. The effect is dramatic yet controlled and makes no impact outside the building envelope. In this quiet, understated way, Wespi and de Meuron provide an alternative to suburban chaos.

1,2 Views of exterior
3   Detail of light well
4   Garage entrance
5   Staircase from garage
6,7 Hallway and kitchen
8   Swimming pool with views of lake
9,10 Living space

3

4

5

6

7

8

9

10

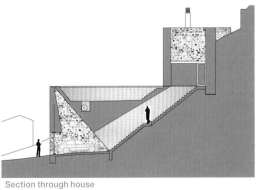

Section through house

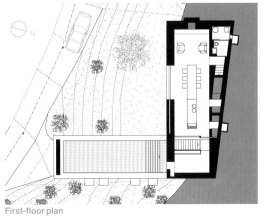

First-floor plan

House SH
Hiroshi Nakamura
& NAP Architects

4

Tokyo, Japan
2005

House SH is a rare commodity in a modern city environment – a new-build home large enough for a family. Intricately knit into a dense Tokyo streetscape, it reflects the scale of neighbouring buildings but is otherwise devoid of residential detail. Instead, it offers an intriguingly blank facade to the street, save for its signature 'bulge'. It does not enter into stylistic conflict with its urban environment but brings a quieter, softer aesthetic into play. This reflects an interior built around the needs of the family and the wider concerns of the architect, who aims to achieve intimacy between architecture and people.

The form of the house — including its swollen facade — has been driven by the desire to create as much space and light as possible on a tight,

north-facing plot. The building is the maximum height achievable and is set out as a series of decks connected vertically by a spiral staircase. The defining feature is the void to the north of the plan, which draws daylight deep into the building from a large light-well in the roof. Throughout the building, space, function and privacy are not defined in conventional terms but by the strength and character of the light.

The second floor, where the deck extends across the plan, is the living and dining hub of the house. Conscious of its importance to modern family life, this is the zone in which the architect has been most innovative in maximizing space, both physically and visually. Largely open-plan, it is focused on

the curved, white bulge that so intrigues from the street. This form is embraced as both sculpture and furniture — a place to relax while light dances playfully around you, creating different moods depending on the time of day. Hiroshi Nakamura has created an architecture with which the family can actively engage.

1   View of house from street
2   Detail of spiral staircase
3   North facade
4,5 Views of living space
6   Detail of light-well
7,8 Interior spiral staircase

5

6

Section through house

First-floor plan

7

Lotus House
Kengo Kuma & Associates

Lotus House is a quiet mountain retreat designed as a weekend getaway from the city. As a sanctuary from the hubbub of daily city life, its commission enabled Kengo Kuma to move away from an architecture of solidity. It is the epitome of designing with a delicate touch, looking more outwards than inwards and providing a place of transition between the mountains and the river.

The house sits comfortably within the tradition of Japanese architecture, which emphasizes horizontal linearity. Divided into two wings, it is laid out as a ribbon of rooms over two floors, with a linking corridor hugging the northern boundary. From the road it is completely unobtrusive but it opens out dramatically on the other side, where it steps down towards the river. From this viewpoint it looks like an intricate chequerboard of solids and voids, with a courtyard and lotus pond as the principal focus. The rhythm established between glass and water, stone and air, blurs boundaries between inside and out. The house appears almost like a pontoon that may one day drift from its mooring.

Kuma's architecture focuses on the use of natural materials, challenging our assumptions about their purpose and properties. In the Lotus House he works extensively with travertine (Italian limestone). Applying more widely the theme of solids and voids to the way the building is clad, he has created a chain mail that naturally lights and ventilates the interior. Thin travertine plates are fastened to a supporting steel skeleton innovatively designed as a flat bar chain structure, meaning that each bar element stays in place by being sandwiched to its neighbours. The system affords flexibility against outer forces and movement. On a more poetic note, it achieves the effect of effortless suspension, drawing parallels between the lightness of the stone and the eponymous lotus petals.

1   Main entrance to house
2   South facade
3   Courtyard overlooking lotus pond
4   First-floor balcony
5   Central courtyard
6   View into courtyard from first floor

3

4

5

6

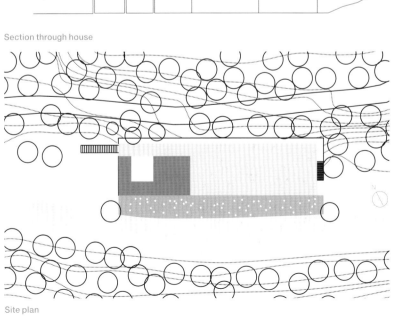

Section through house

Site plan

Slice House
Procter:Rihl

Slice House is a city residence for a sociable single occupant with a love of entertaining. It derives its name from the long, narrow infill plot that it occupies in a built-up suburb of Porto Alegre. Appropriate to a city where most people are of European descent, the building is a conscious hybrid of Brazilian and British influences that marries open-plan and extrovert with enclosed and discreet. It is an undulating asymmetric design that has been crafted using local construction techniques and is responsive to climate and context, yet formally unique.

The awkward site overlooked by tower blocks provided a challenge to the brief for a light and airy building with private outdoor space. The response is a house with a simple linear plan that is transformed in three dimensions through illusion. The architect's wider interest in complex geometries is exploited to create the feeling of greater space through the angling of walls and ceilings. The house also draws in light in unexpected ways. The ground floor is essentially one long room, incorporating a large covered courtyard. It has a dramatic sense of depth and is atmospherically lit by its chief design feature — the transparent volume of the swimming pool. Upstairs, the folding concrete ceiling expands and contracts, suggesting a difference in scale and ambience between the private and social areas.

The house is of reinforced concrete construction, built using a local timber-formed pouring technique. The exterior expresses the duality of the design, with expanses of raw concrete matched by British precision in the detailing of steel elements, including sun-shading grilles and the entire entrance facade. Internally, the architect's trademark integrated furniture is used to enhance the free-flowing nature of the space. The signature element is a 7 m (23 ft) long counter, which serves as dining table, worktop and garden ledge.

1   Aerial view of house
2   View from street
3   Seating area and pool
4   View of living space
5,6 Pool terrace
7   Interior staircase

3

4

5

6

7

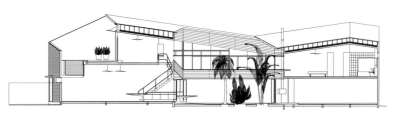

Section through house

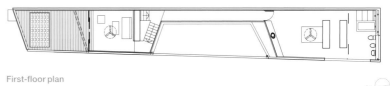

First-floor plan

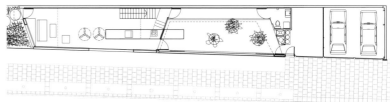

Ground-floor plan

Solar Umbrella House
Pugh + Scarpa Architects

1

2

Solar Umbrella House is the extension and reinvention of a 1920s bungalow as an exemplary home for sustainable twenty-first century living. Designed by a married couple for themselves and their young son, it typifies the exploratory nature of Pugh+Scarpa's work. In blurring the boundaries between indoor and outdoor space, it takes forwards the concerns of earlier California modernists and exploits them for both aesthetic and environmental gain. It draws inspiration from Paul Rudolph's Umbrella House, where a sun-shading canopy gives the building its graceful and iconic form.

The house is set on a long, narrow through-plot in a low-rise suburban neighbourhood. The extension transforms the original building into a spacious two-storey residence, reorientated to face south. It now has a lighter appearance, with the interior arranged so that views, air and space are free-flowing. A new entrance porch, with master suite above, is set discretely to one side so that at its highest point the building has minimal impact on neighbours. The centre-piece is the southeast elevation, which is fully glazed and retractable at ground-floor level.

Throughout the house, various elements have key roles to play in both creating a signature look and supporting environmental performance. For example, the canopy of solar panels, which wraps around the south elevation and roof terrace, creates an abstract composition with its supporting walls and screens. It not only shades the building but absorbs the sunlight, generating all the electricity required to run the house. Inside, a palette of recycled and functional materials is used, whilst light is specifically trained on exposed surfaces of steel, chipboard and Homasote (panels of compressed recycled paper) to create a vibrant interior.

1 House in context
2 View from garden
3 Living space
4 Southeast facade
5 Dining area
6 Master bedroom
7 Patio and solar panel canopy

3

103

5

6

7

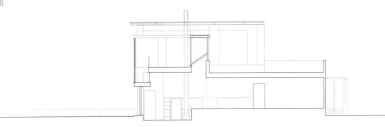

Section through house

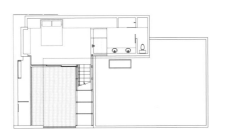

First-floor plan

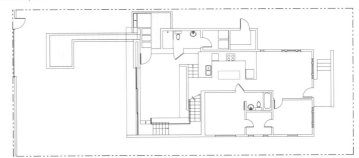

Ground-floor plan

St Andrews Beach House
Sean Godsell Architects

Mornington Peninsula, Victoria, Australia
2005

St Andrews Beach House is a holiday residence, commissioned by a client keen to re-engage with nature. It is set on a stretch of coastline where building is permitted right at the water's edge. With an informal, fluid approach to space and the protection of an outer shell, the building responds to an exposed waterfront site with magnificent views. It also sits within the wider context of Sean Godsell's research into evolving Australian architecture and references the traditional outback homestead in its deliberate ambiguity between inside and outside.

The building is a three-bedroom family home laid out over one floor. The simple rectangular plan is divided into two distinct halves — shared and private. There is an open-plan living space at the sea end and a suite of bedrooms and bathrooms to the rear. As requested in the client's brief, there is no internal means of circulation. Each room is accessed off a covered walkway, which is an outside space within the building envelope. At each end of the walkway there is in an open gallery, while a sliced breezeway divides the two zones. Moving through the house is a voyage of transition between inside and outside, which reflects the architect's interest in what he calls 'abstracted veranda space'.

To maximize views from the elevated site, the house is raised on columns. Its legibility as a singular object is enhanced by the unbroken outer skin, which is made of oxidized steel industrial floor grating. With operable hinged panels that act as a *brise-soleil* (or sun shade), the highly durable envelope mediates between the exposed coastal site and the interior. It acts as a filter, tempering harsh extremes of weather while naturally ventilating the house. As an aesthetic device, it also creates a frame for the fully glazed west elevation, which opens up to bring the stunning seascape indoors.

1,2	Oxidized steel exterior
3	View of living space
4	South facade
5,6	Details of exterior
7	Top of entrance staircase
8,9	Living spaces
10	View to coast from interior

3

4

5

6

7

8

9

10

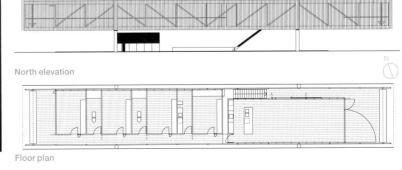

North elevation

Floor plan

Tóló House
Alvaro Leite Siza Vieira

1

2

Tóló House is nestled deep in the mountainous terrain of northern Portugal. Its fragmented, abstract form derives directly from the landscape, a place so loved by the client that he wanted to build a summerhouse there, despite limited means. The challenge for the architect was to unlock the potential of a beautiful but highly restrictive site to accommodate a workable family building on a modest budget. He has succeeded by taking clues from the inherent nature of the topography, creating a building that does not simply sit on the site but runs in, over and through it.

The plan is based on the most rational and economic use of the plot, which is steep, long and narrow. Avoiding intrusive groundworks that would change its character completely meant finding a way of embracing the incline. The building is not a single unified volume but a sinuous waterfall of small interconnected modules partially buried in the hillside. Each individual unit has a distinct domestic use: living room, bedroom, office, and so on. These are clearly visible through large picture windows on the myriad concrete planes that together form the south elevation. In contrast, the north elevation is not a facade at all but a blank concrete platform thrusting out to embrace the view.

The building is underpinned by geometric rigour as it twists down the hillside, setting three bedrooms at an angle to the slope. This provides the requisite privacy within an integrated interior that includes a generous open-plan living space. Linked by rhythmic external steps running the full length of the site, roof planes double as patios and place the house within a wider vernacular tradition. They serve to animate the exterior with human activity, creating a sociable building that is highly efficient in its use of every available level.

1   Hillside site
2   Exterior from south
3   Living area
4,5 Details of exterior and patios
6   Interior stairs
7,8 Views of living space

3

4

5

Tóló House
Alvaro Leite Siza Vieira

7

6

8

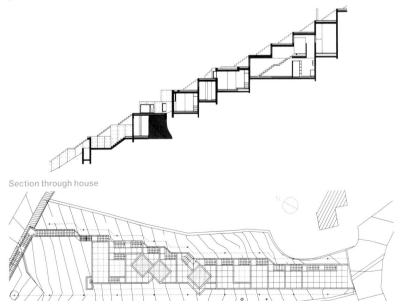

Section through house

Site plan

Wheatsheaf House
Jesse Judd Architects

Intended as a family holiday home, Wheatsheaf House is an intriguing and witty response to its forested surroundings that echoes traditional Australian vernacular buildings.

Set in a small clearing within an abandoned Eucalyptus plantation, the house consists of two C-shaped volumes set side by side. The structure is a ribcage of steel frames, wrapped in black corrugated steel and lined with glowing orange-stained plywood. The use of corrugated steel recalls the utilitarian lean-to sheds and farm buildings that are so common in the area. The house sits on a plinth that elevates it several centimetres above the ground and the ends of the building and the mouth of the C are filled by full-height, glazed walls and sliding doors.

The larger of the two volumes contains an open living and dining area and kitchen, the smaller houses a neat arrangement of three bedrooms and a bathroom connected by a corridor. The curving form of the house blurs distinctions between floors, wall and roof; each blends into the next in a warm, comfortable continuity of stained wood. The shape of the house is central to its relationship with its setting; while snugly enclosing the interior space, it still allows the occupants a panoramic view of their forest location. A reclaimed-timber deck that surrounds the house provides further opportunity for enjoyment of the landscape, whilst its raised position ensures that the house has a minimal physical impact upon its environment and wildlife

can run freely beneath. The raised position of the structure also encourages the notion that it could be picked-up and relocated elsewhere with relative ease, a visual pun on the holiday home brief.

1   View from north
2   View from east
3   Living space with view of forest
4   Curved steel exterior
5   External deck
6,7 Views of living space

3

5

6

7

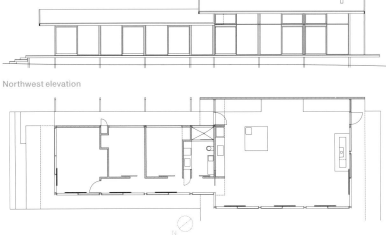

Northwest elevation

Floor plan

Fink House
Dietrich Untertrifaller Architekten

The Fink House belongs to an emerging Alpine house type. It is set in Bregenzerwald, in Austria's Vorarlberg province, an area with a high concentration of good quality architecture. While drawing from the vernacular, it offers a peaceful haven for the modern family — reflecting a cultural shift away from an agricultural way of life to one based on leisure and tourism. The house is respectful of its context. In particular, Fink House aligns itself with the architectural tradition of the Vorarlberg in its integration of a range of spaces and functions into one compact form, and in the economic use of silver fir to clad the exterior.

Fink House is laid out over three levels, following the contours of the sloping site to incorporate a self-contained apartment on the lower floor, with the main house above. There are a number of exterior spaces, such as a terrace to the apartment and two ribbons of decking. Like the ground-floor garage, they are integrated into the rectangular footprint of the building, made possible by exploiting the structural qualities of a timber frame. It preserves the integrity of the overall form and gives the building its signature look — a dynamic interplay of planes and voids, presence and absence.

Influenced by the tactile qualities of vernacular pitched-roof housing, the finely detailed facades of Fink House are a rhythmic mix of untreated laths of silver fir and continuous ribbon glazing. Further differentiation between the planes and voids is achieved through the use of silver fir veneer in the recesses. Internally, the horizontal emphasis is developed in an open-plan arrangement of dining, living and library areas on the upper floor. The sense of the house as an object in the landscape extends to all design details, from the uninterrupted walnut surfaces to the handles and roller shutters.

1   View from southwest
2   West facade
3   Upper-floor dining area
4   South facade
5   Detail of staircase
6   Upper-floor living space
7   View from terrace

3

119

4

5

6

7

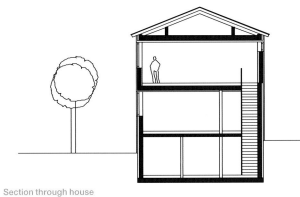

Section through house

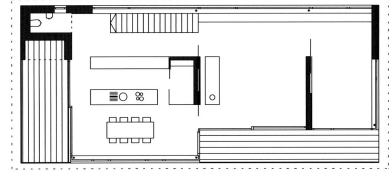

First-floor plan

Maison E
Shigeru Ban Architects

Maison E is a private residence designed to meet the evolving needs of an extended family. Situated on a stretch of coast two hours north of Tokyo, it occupies the highest point of a quiet suburban site, adjacent to a communal apartment block. Based on a rigorous grid system, it typifies the rationality of Shigeru Ban and his interest in the logical geometry of western modernism. It combines a lean architectural approach with a Japanese sensibility to create the optimum living environment — a delicate equilibrium between private and public, inside and outside.

At 1,200 m² (12,916 sq ft) the house is a notably large building for its type but retains a sense of intimacy of scale through the careful proportioning of its individual spaces. Laid out over two storeys, it has a consciously inward-looking plan that minimizes the effects of activity from the surrounding streetscape. It is arranged as a group of lightweight steel pavilions around a central boulevard, which brings light and air into the heart of the building. Coherency is maintained by the excellent sightlines and underlying geometry of the plan, which is generated from a strict grid of small and large squares.

Maison E was commissioned by the owner of a fashion company and, stylistically, is both timeless and understated. Within its footprint, the architect has incorporated a range of outdoor spaces, including a swimming pool, courtyards and gardens. Continuing a particularly Japanese concern with the partitioning of space, the structural steel skeleton is filled in with a patchwork of panels: opaque, translucent, transparent and void. This provides screening only where privacy is required, thus preserving the family dynamic and creating a shifting perspective on the captivating mountain views.

1   View of entrance courtyard
2   East facade
3   View through internal courtyard
4   Northeast corner of house
5,6 Views of living space
7   Swimming pool courtyard
8   Bathroom

3

Maison E
Shigeru Ban Architects

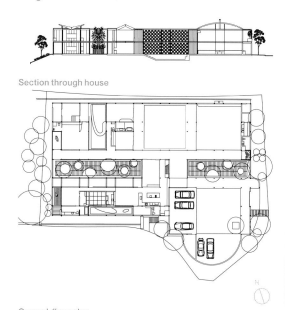

Section through house

Ground-floor plan

4

5

6

7

8

Mimetic House
Dominic Stevens Architect

Mimetic relates to the nature of imitation or mimicry. In the case of Dominic Stevens' tiny rural dwelling, it perfectly sums up the presence of the building as a constantly changing mirror to the mountainous Irish landscape. In Stevens' work there is an overall concern with the engagement between responsible new architecture and a productive, living environment. Quietly nestling in a working pasture, Mimetic House is the epitome of his ideas, where the rich texture of the farmland setting has an impact on the built form, rather than the other way round.

The house is a modest building, both physically and economically. It was designed for a pair of conceptual artists with a limited budget, who wished to live and work in the countryside. Laid out over two floors, it is conceived of as two spatially distinct volumes — 'earthwork' and 'framework' — with a marked difference in ambience. The lower floor is partially embedded in the earth: a protective environment for sleeping, bathing and contemplative working. The upper floor is a flexible, open-plan, angular space for living, eating, socializing and artistic collaboration. The two are connected by a reinforced concrete column that wraps around the only means of vertical circulation — a sculptural spiral staircase.

The tilted walls of the upper live/work space are irregular planes, each a rhythmic composition of alternating solids and voids. The contrast between white walls and glazing creates a consciously disorientating interior with filtered, abstract views of the surrounding hills and a mood that changes in response to the weather. Externally, the opaque portions are clad with mirrored glass and are angled to reflect more land than sky. This transforms the building into a ghost-like presence, by day almost invisible and by night aglow with radiant internal light.

1,2 Exterior views of house
3   Living space
4   Detail of exterior
5   External view at dusk
6   View from study window
7   Kitchen

3

4

5

6

7

Section through house

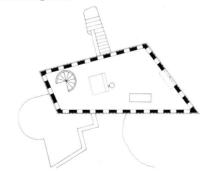

Ground-floor plan

Ring House
Makoto Takei + Chie Nabeshima / TNA

Ring House
Makoto Takei + Chie
Nabeshima / TNA

Karuizawa, Nagano Prefecture, Japan
2006

Karuizawa is a community of over 300 homes in an idyllic woodland setting. Developed speculatively for the weekender market three hours drive northwest of Tokyo, it offers a peaceful retreat for city dwellers. In accepting a commission to design a house in Karuizawa, the architects took on a difficult plot with a steep terrain and dense forest views, but they have interpreted these challenges as opportunities and enjoyed the freedom of designing outside the urban context. Unconstrained by issues such as privacy, the architects have capitalized on the concept of an object in the round. The name of the house not only has arboreal connotations — it perfectly sums up a building that is at the quiet centre of a particular and intimate natural context.

The exact position of the house was influenced by factors such as coding guidelines and boundary issues but principally by the delicate ecology of the landscape. The building is the maximum permissible height and stands on the crest of the site, assuming a slender, vertical profile on a compact grid footprint. With a partially sunken basement level, it is laid out over three storeys plus roof terrace, but this is not easily read from outside.

A conventional understanding of the interior has been obscured by the 'ring'— the design concept based on the rhythmic composition of the facades and the dynamic interplay of solids and voids. Each elevation is identical, articulated in contrasting bands of cedar and glass that wrap round the light-weight ramen wood frame. Floor slabs are hidden behind the solid planes, as are bespoke functional elements such as the kitchen counter and stove. The overall effect is of a single composition, with no discernible front or back. The horizontal emphasis interplays beautifully with the scale and proportion of the house, while uninterrupted views through the structure preserve the character of the existing forest.

1   Detail of cedar rings
2,3 Views of exterior
4   House in context
5   Living space
6   Bathroom with sunken bath

3

4

5

6

Section through house

Ground-floor plan

House in Pego
Siza Vieira Arquiteto

On an elevated site overlooking the coastal resort of Praia Grande, House in Pego is a large five-bedroom family home. While its long, low profile and branching layout create a marked contrast with neighbouring holiday villas, the building is undoubtedly in keeping with the local topography. Its stepped design follows the contours of the plot (which drops away towards the sea) and extensive use is made of both timber and stone, as well as roof-top planting. The jagged plan may be a departure for the 'rational' Siza Vieira, but the strong sense of place is very much in keeping with the rest of his work.

Laid out over a single storey (but with four subtle changes in level), the house's floorplan resembles a flower, with rooms as leaves sprouting from a central stem. From the discreet main entrance to the south, the visitor is channelled along a narrow corridor with a small room off to the left and two to the right. Beyond this space, the flower opens up to reveal a total of six rooms branching off in various directions. The layout appears erratic, but has an underlying sense of order. Bedrooms are to the east of the stem, with gaps between them, while the living and kitchen areas overlap to the west, opening onto terraces and a swimming pool.

The building is made of loadbearing masonry and clad with smooth stone and treated timber. The vertical wooden batons accentuate the house's many angles and reinforce the cubic shape of the various volumes. The rhythm that they establish is maintained by folding timber screens that protect glazed double doors to every room. On the whim of the occupants, absolute privacy can be achieved or the house can be opened up to magnificently framed sea views and a landscaped garden.

1   Main entrance
2   West facade
3   Living area with timber screen
4   View across roof from north
5   Swimming pool and terraces
6,7 Exterior views and shutters
8,9 Views of living space
10 Dining area

3

4

5

6

7

8

9

10

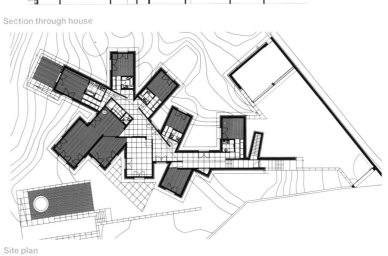

Section through house

Site plan

House O
Sou Fujimoto Architects

1

2

Situated on the rocky Tateyama coastline, two hours south of Tokyo, House O is a weekend hideaway and gateway to the Pacific. With a blank facade to the road and a glazed one to the ocean, it mediates between the built and natural worlds. Its simplicity of form disguises an underlying rigour that sets up magnificent sea views in a cinematic way. This creates a spatial experience that is orchestrated yet intimate and that constantly changes within the understated, finely detailed interior.

The house is laid out over a single level and occupies nearly the full width of the site. The plan is geometric but highly irregular and branch-like. Private areas are located at the outer edges of the 'tree', with space becoming more fluid towards the central living and dining core. As there are no internal partitions, the transition between zones is seamless and long views are established right through the space. In the secluded northern corners, slot skylights provide additional daylight and create atmospheric interiors. This is in contrast to the sense of openness achieved to the south, where the house embraces the ocean through full-height frameless glazed walls.

House O is a room without borders. It celebrates the comfortable 'in-between' spaces that are the hub of contemporary life. The idea of seamlessness runs throughout the project, from the overall plan to the smallest of details. As far as possible, surfaces are kept free and continuous by the concealment of openings and integration of fittings. Materials have been chosen for the possibilities that they offer in creating different moods, depending on their application and finish. Concrete is used extensively: rough and tactile on the exterior, smooth and polished within. Tatami flooring ties the house to the Japanese context, just as glass provides the link to the immediate surroundings.

1 View from coast
2 Detail of east facade
3 View of living space
4 Closed west facade
5 Open plan-interior
6,7 Interior spaces showing coastal view

3

4

5

6

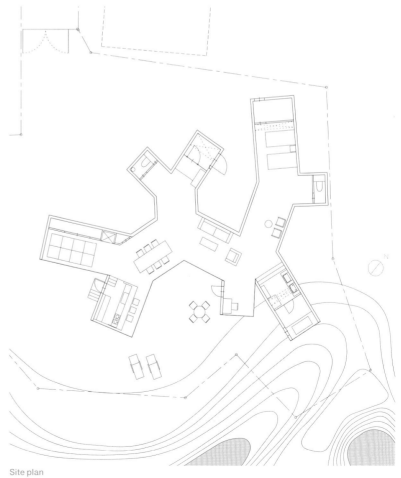

7

Site plan

Villa 1
Powerhouse Company

The first major project of an emerging design practice, Villa 1 is described by its creators as an 'upside down' house. To maximize space while meeting local regulations on height and volume, it is laid out over two floors of equal size — one above ground, one below. The inversion derives from placing public rooms over private, making a creative distinction between rooms for day and those for night. The contrast between light and shade informs all aspects of the design, from the layout of the arrowhead plan to the exquisite detail of integrated fittings and materials.

The house is located in a man-made forest, with trees on all sides. So that each living space can enjoy sweeping views and benefit from natural light, the building is laid out in a distinctive Y-shaped plan. This subverts conventional ideas of the front and back of a house, creating an egalitarian space that radiates out from a central 'melting pot' of hall, dining room and bar. Of the three wings, one is given over to work and master suite, one to cooking and garage space and one to relaxing and guest rooms. There are covered terraces to the south and east and a patio to let in light.

The villa is tailored to its owner's eclectic tastes, with an extreme contrast in mood between floors. On the upper level, a concealed steel frame supports a completely glazed envelope with a sliding marble door. A bookcase in the north wing doubles as a truss. Services and structural elements are contained within three pieces of custom-made furniture in wood, slate and concrete respectively. These are used instead of walls to loosely partition space. By contrast, the lower floor is carved out of cast concrete, with vaulted ceilings and thick walls creating an intimate riposte to the openness above.

1,2   House in context
3,4   Views of exterior
5   Garage
6,7   Views of retaining wall
8   Detail of living area
9   View into house from garden
10   Living area

3

4

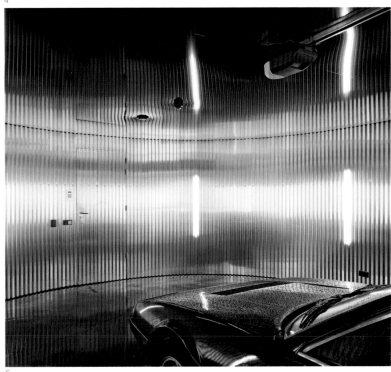

5

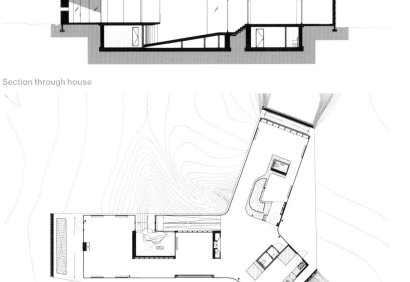

Section through house

Site plan

7

6

8

9

10

Villa NM
UNStudio

Villa NM is a family home set in extensive woodland two hours north of New York. The area has become increasingly popular as a seasonal retreat from the city and the NM client typify its younger urbanite homeowners. They came to the project with clear ideas about the look and feel of their summerhouse and the rationale behind its design. They wanted a building both bold and respectful, a home with the geometric rigour of mid-century modernism that would sit lightly in the rural landscape and capitalize on spectacular views in-the-round.

The elastic form of the building and spatial organization generate from the natural slope of the extensive hilltop site. Continuing the concerns of the earlier Möbius House (1998), the architect has taken a simple box-like shell and twisted it into two separate volumes within one continuous skeleton. In a sinuous sweep up the incline, the lower volume hugs the ground while the upper one is raised on slender columns. The pivotal midpoint is formed by a set of five parallel planes in rotation, so walls become floors and vice versa. This complex form is based on simple geometric repetition and has allowed for structural off-site pre-fabrication.

The split-level interior is articulated in smooth sculptural curves that resonate with the rolling landscape. Core functions are centred in the vertical axis, leaving the outer walls free to play out the relationship between dark concrete, gold-tinted glass and glowing polycarbonate. As the building ascends the slope, the views gradually reveal themselves and in the living room space are harnessed in a full wall panorama. The openness of the space confirms that this is the social hub of the house, its literal and lyrical turning point which signals the transition from public to private.

1   East corner at night
2   Northwest facade
3   View of staircase from living room
4   Cantilevered exterior
5   Glazed northeast facade
6   Southeast facade at night
7   View of living space

3

4

5

New York, USA
2007

6

7

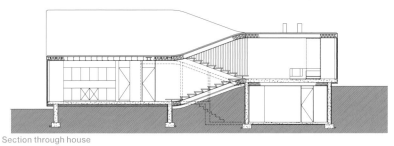

Section through house

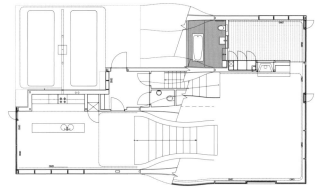

Floor plan

Index

2-Parts House, 30
24 H-architecture, Dragspel House, 46

Aires Mateus, House on the Coast, 62
Andreas Fuhrimann, Gabrielle Hächler Architekten,
    Holiday House on the Rigi, 58
Argentina, San Isidro, Buenos Aires, Casa Ponce, 34
Årjäng, Sweden, Dragspel House, 46
Australia,
Dover Heights, New South Wales, Holman House, 82
Kangaloon, New South Wales, Kangaloon House, 6
Melbourne, 2-Parts House, 30
Mornington Peninsula, Victoria, St Andrews Beach
    House, 106
Victoria, Wheatsheaf House, 114
Austria, Bezau, Bregenz, Fink House, 118

Bahia Azul, Los Vilos, Chile, Casa Larrain, 22
Baron House, 66
Bennekom, Ede, The Netherlands, Villa 1, 142
Bezau, Bregenz, Austria, Fink House, 118
BKK Architects, 2-Parts House, 30
Brazil,
Paraty, Rio de Janeiro, Du Plessis House, 38
Porto Alegre, Rio Grande do Sul, Slice House, 98
Ribeirão Preto, São Paulo, House in Ribeirão Preto, 10
Brick House, 70
Brione, Locarno, Switzerland, House in Brione, 86

California,
Pacific Palisades, Santa Monica, Hill House, 54
Venice, Santa Monica, Solar Umbrella House, 102
Caruso St John, Brick House, 70
Casa Larrain, 22
Casa Ponce, 34
Chiba Prefecture, Japan, House O, 138
Chichibu, Saitama Prefecture, Japan, Fireworks
    House, 78
Chile, Bahia Azul, Casa Larrain, 22
China, Shaanxi Province, Father's House in Jade
    Mountains, 42

Delta Shelter, 74
Dietrich Untertrifaller Architekten, Fink House, 118

Dominic Stevens Architect, Mimetic House, 126
Dover Heights, New South Wales, Australia,
    Holman House, 82
Dragspel House, 46
Dromahair, County Leitrim, Republic of Ireland,
    Mimetic House, 126
Du Plessis House, 38
Durbach Block Architects, Holman House, 82

Father's House in Jade Mountains, 42
Fink House, 118
Fireworks House, 78

Goodman House, 50

Hadano, Kanagawa Prefecture, Japan, Roof
    House, 14
Hill House, 54
Hiroshi Nakamura & NAP Architects, House SH, 90
Holiday House on the Rigi, 58
Holman House, 82
House in Brione, 86
House in Pego, Siza Vieira Arquiteto, Praia Grande,
    Portugal, 134
House in Ribeirão Preto, 10
House O, 138
House on the Coast, 62
House SH, 90

Iwaki, Fukushima Prefecture, Japan, Maison E, 122

Japan,
Chiba Prefecture, House O, 138
Chichibu, Saitama Prefecture, Fireworks House, 78
Hadano, Kanagawa Prefecture, Roof House, 18
Iwaki, Fukushima Prefecture, Maison E, 122
Kanagawa Prefecture, Lotus House, 94
Karuizawa, Nagano Prefecture, Ring House, 130
Shiga Prefecture, Springtecture B House, 26
Tokyo, House SH, 90
Jesse Judd Architects, Wheatsheaf House, 114
Johnston Marklee & Associates, Hill House, 54

Kanagawa Prefecture, Japan, Lotus House, 94
Kangaloon House, 6
Kangaloon, New South Wales, Australia, 6
Karuizawa, Nagano Prefecture, Japan, Ring
    House, 130
Kengo Kuma & Associates, Lotus House, 94
Klotz, Mathias, Casa Ponce, 34
Kogan, Márcio, Du Plessis House, 38
Årjäng, Sweden, Dragspel House, 46

Litoral Alentejano, Portugal, House on the Coast, 62
London, UK,
The Red House, 14
Brick House, 70
Lotus House, 94

MADA s.p.a.m., Father's House in Jade
    Mountains, 42
Maison E, 122
Makoto Takei + Chie Nabeshima / TNA, Ring
    House, 130
Markus Wespi Jérôme de Meuron Architects,
    House in Brione, 86
Mazama, Washington, USA, Delta Shelter, 74
Melbourne, Australia, 2-Parts House, 30
Mimetic House, 126
MMBB / SPBR, House in Ribeirão Preto, 10
Mornington Peninsula, St Andrews Beach
    House, 106

Nagano Prefecture, Japan, Ring House, 94
Nendo Inc, Fireworks House, 78
The Netherlands, Bennekom, Ede, Villa 1, 142
New South Wales,
Kangaloon, Kangaloon House, 6
Dover Heights, Holman House, 82
New York, USA
Pine Plains, Goodman House, 50
Villa NM, 146

Olson Sundberg Kundig Allen Architects,
    Delta Shelter, 74

Pacific Palisades, Santa Monica, California, USA, Hill House, 54
Paraty, Rio de Janeiro, Brazil, Du Plessis House, 38
Pawson, John, Baron House, 66
Pine Plains, New York, USA, Goodman House, 50
Porto Alegre, Rio Grande do Sul, Brazil, Slice House, 98
Portugal,
Litoral Alentejano, House on the Coast, 62
Praia Grande, House in Pego, 134
Vila Real, Porto, Tóló House, 110
Powerhouse Company, Villa 1, 142
Praia Grande, Portugal, House in Pego, 134
Preston Scott Cohen, Goodman House, 50
Procter:Rihl, Slice House, 98
Puga, Cecilia Larrain, Casa Larrain, 22
Pugh+Scarpa Architects, Solar Umbrella House, 102

The Red House, 14
Republic of Ireland, Dromahair, County Leitrim, Mimetic House, 126
Ribeirão Preto, São Paulo, Brazil, House in Ribeirão Preto, 10
Rigi Scheidegg, Gersau, Switzerland, Holiday House on the Rigi, 58
Ring House, 130
Roof House, 18

St Andrews Beach House, 106
San Isidro, Buenos Aires, Argentina, Casa Ponce, 34
Sean Godsell Architects, St Andrews Beach House, 106
Shaanxi Province, Father's House in Jade Mountains, 42
Shiga Prefecture, Japan, Springtecture B House, 26
Shigeru Ban Architects, Maison E, 122
Shuhei Endo Architect Institute, Springtecture B House, 26
Siza Vieira Arquiteto, House in Pego, 134
Siza, Alvaro Leite Vieira, Tóló House, 110
Skåne, Sweden, Baron House, 66
Slice House, 98
Solar Umbrella House, 102
Sou Fujimoto Architects, House O, 138
Springtecture B House, 26

Sweden,
Årjäng, Dragspel House, 46
Skåne, Baron House, 66
Switzerland,
Brione, Locarno, House in Brione, 86
Rigi Scheidegg, Gersau, Holiday House on the Rigi, 58

Tezuka Architects, Roof House, 18
Tokyo, Japan, House SH, 90
Tóló House, 110
Tony Fretton Architects, The Red House, 14

UK,
London, The Red House, 14
London, Brick House, 70
UNStudio, Villa NM, 146
USA,
Mazama, Washington, Delta Shelter, 74
New York, Villa NM, 146
Pacific Palisades, Santa Monica, California, Hill House, 54
Pine Plains, New York, Goodman House, 50
Venice, Santa Monica, California, Solar Umbrella House, 102

Victoria, Australia, Wheatsheaf House, 114
Vila Real, Porto, Portugal, Tóló House, 110
Villa 1, 142
Villa NM, 146

Washington, USA, Mazama, Delta Shelter, 74
Wheatsheaf House, 114

Picture credits
Anthony Browell: pp.6–9, Peter Durant: pp.14–15, p.17 (7,9), ©Helene
Binet: p.16, p.17(8), pp.70-74, ©Katsuhisa Kida: pp.18–21, Cristobal
Palma: pp.22–25, Shannon McGrath: pp.30–33, Arnaldo Pappalardo:
pp.38–41, Roland Halbe: pp.34–37, Christian Richters: pp.42–45,
Victoria Sambunaris: pp.50–53, Eric Staudenmaier: pp.54–57, Valentin
Jeck: pp.58–61, DMF Fotografia: pp.62–65, Fabien Baron: pp.66–69,
Benjamin Benschneider: pp.74–77, Tim Bies, Olson Sundberg Kundig
Allen: pp.74–77, Daici Ano: pp.78–81, 90–93, 94–97, 130–133, 138–141,
Reiner Blunck: p.82, Brett Boardman: pp.82–85, Marcelo Nunes: pp.98–
101, Sue Barr: pp.98–101, Marvin Rand: pp.102–105, Earl Carter: pp.106–
109, Duccio Malagamba: pp.110–113, 134–137, Bruno Klomfar: pp.118–
121, Hiroyuki Hirai: pp.122–125, Ros Kavanagh: pp.126–129, Christian
Richters: pp.146–149, Bas Princen: pp.142–145

Phaidon Press Limited
Regent's Wharf
All Saints Street
London N1 9PA

Phaidon Press Inc.
180 Varick Street
New York, NY 10014

www.phaidon.com

©2009 Phaidon Press Limited

ISBN: 978 0 7148 5599 8

A CIP catalogue record for this book is available
from the British Library.

Text by Máire Cox
Designed by Hans Stofregen
Printed in China